HAL•LEONARD

INSTRUMENTAL PLAY-ALONG

AUDIO ACCESS INCLUDED

PLAYBACK+
Speed • Pitch • Balance • Loop

CELLO

T0088518

IRISH FAVORITES

CONTENTS

To access audio visit:
www.halleonard.com/mylibrary

Enter Code
3374-7415-7065-6243

ISBN 978-1-4234-9533-8

HAL•LEONARD CORPORATION

7777 W. BLUEMOUND RD. P.O. BOX 13819 MILWAUKEE, WI 53213

Visit Hal Leonard Online at
www.halleonard.com

BELIEVE ME, IF ALL THOSE
ENDEARING YOUNG CHARMS

Words and Music by
THOMAS MOORE

CELLO

THE BELLS OF ST. MARY'S

CELLO

Words by DOUGLAS FURBER
Music by A. EMMETT ADAMS

BLACK VELVET BAND

CELLO

Traditional

BRENNAN ON THE MOOR

CELLO

Traditional

COCKLES AND MUSSELS
(Molly Malone)

CELLO

Traditional

THE CROPPY BOY

CELLO

18th Century Irish Folksong

DANNY BOY

CELLO

Words by FREDERICK EDWARD WEATHERLY
Traditional Irish Folk Melody

EASY AND SLOW

CELLO

Traditional

THE FOGGY DEW

CELLO

Traditional

GREEN GROW THE RUSHES, O

CELLO

Traditional

THE HUMOUR IS ON ME NOW

CELLO

Traditional

I ONCE LOVED A LASS

CELLO

Traditional

I'LL TAKE YOU HOME AGAIN, KATHLEEN

CELLO

Words and Music by
THOMAS WESTENDORF

I'LL TELL ME MA

CELLO

Traditional

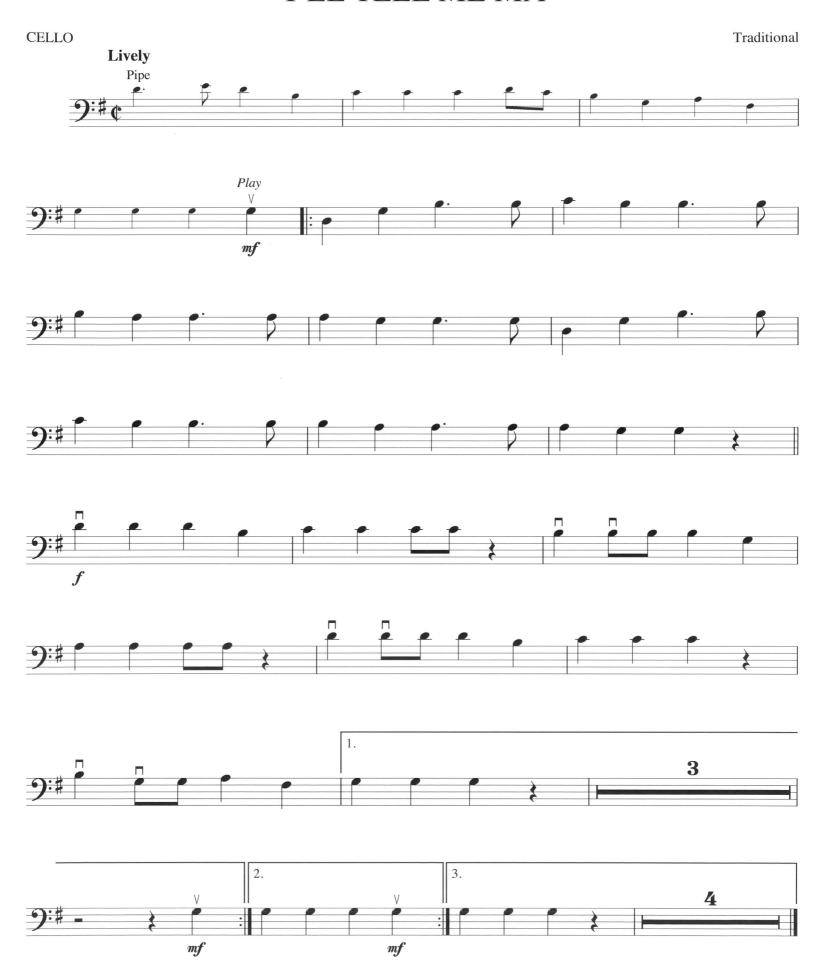

THE IRISH ROVER

CELLO

Traditional

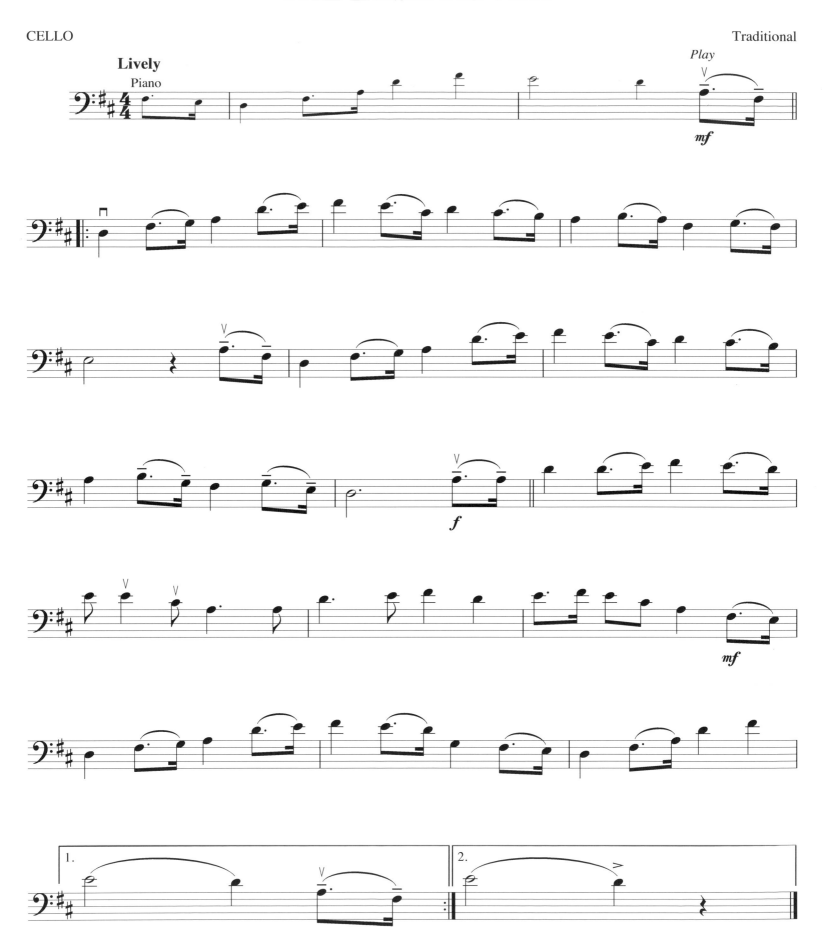

THE JOLLY BEGGARMAN

CELLO

Traditional

THE LITTLE BEGGARMAN

CELLO

Traditional

MacNAMARA'S BAND

CELLO

Words by JOHN J. STAMFORD
Music by SHAMUS O'CONNOR

MINSTREL BOY

CELLO

Traditional

MY WILD IRISH ROSE

CELLO

Words and Music by
CHAUNCEY OLCOTT

Waltz

A NATION ONCE AGAIN

CELLO

Words and Music by
THOMAS DAVIS

THE OLD ORANGE FLUTE

CELLO

Traditional

THE PATRIOT GAME

CELLO

Traditional

RED IS THE ROSE

CELLO

Irish Folksong

THE RISING OF THE MOON

CELLO

Traditional

THE ROSE OF TRALEE

CELLO

Words by C. MORDAUNT SPENCER
Music by CHARLES W. GLOVER

TOO-RA-LOO-RA-LOO-RAL
(That's an Irish Lullabye)

CELLO

Words and Music by
JAMES R. SHANNON

THE WEARING OF THE GREEN

CELLO

18th Century Irish Folksong

WHEN IRISH EYES ARE SMILING

CELLO

Words by CHAUNCEY OLCOTT
and GEORGE GRAFF, JR.
Music by ERNEST R. BALL

THE WILD COLONIAL BOY

CELLO

Traditional

WILD ROVER

CELLO

Traditional